MORGAN ROSE was born in New Orleans, grew up in New Mexico, and currently lives in Melbourne. She is an internationally produced playwright and performance maker. Her work is contemporary and darkly funny, with an element of absurdism. In addition to her text-based work she has a background in physical theatre and devising. She has studied with SITI Company (NYC, USA), Pacific Performance Project (Seattle, USA), Zen Zen Zo Physical Theatre (Brisbane, Australia), and Dairakudakan (Hakuba, Japan). She completed a Master of Writing for Performance at VCA in 2013. In 2020 she was a dramaturgy placement with Malthouse Theatre as part of the Besen Family Artist Program. She was a recipient of the INK writing commission with Red Stitch Actors Theatre in 2014 and again in 2018. Recent works include *Virgins and Cowboys* (writer, Theatreworks, Griffin Theatre), *F.* (writer, Riot Stage/ Poppyseed Festival), *Lord Willing and the Creek Don't Rise* (writer, MKA/MTC NEON), *The BachelorS17E05* (co-creator, La Mama), and *desert, 6:29pm* (writer, Red Stitch/Wuzhen Festival). She is currently the resident writer at Riot Stage Youth Theatre (riotstage. com) and a co-founder of the dramaturgy initiative Lonely Company (lonelycompany.com). She is left handed.

*Keely Woods, Issy Salisbury and Mary-Helen Buchan in the 2017
Queensland Academy of Creative Industries production in Brisbane.
(Photo: Craig English)*

little girls alone in the woods

MORGAN ROSE

CURRENCY PRESS
The performing arts publisher

CURRENCY PLAYS

First published in 2020
by Currency Press Pty Ltd,
PO Box 2287, Strawberry Hills, NSW, 2012, Australia
enquiries@currency.com.au
www.currency.com.au

Typeset by Dean Nottle for Currency Press.
Cover image and design by Alissa Dinalo.

Currency Press acknowledges the Traditional Owners of the Country on which
we live and work. We pay our respects to all Aboriginal and Torres Strait
Islander Elders, past and present.

NATIONAL
LIBRARY
OF AUSTRALIA

A catalogue record for this
book is available from the
National Library of Australia

Contents

Indiah Morris as Alina in the 2017 Queensland Academy of Creative Industries production in Brisbane. (Photo: Craig English)

INTRODUCTION

The title of Morgan Rose's play is an evocative and loaded one. It immediately asks the question of these 'little girls': why are they out there in the woods, and what are they doing?

There is also, intriguingly, an implied sense of impending danger. Is it the word 'little', implying innocence? Or 'girls', with its implication of the weaker sex? Or 'woods', where there is a lack of civilisation? For me it's the word 'alone' that gives a creeping sense of dread.

Young people alone? They could be doing anything! Or at the very least, they could be doing all the things that the rest of us want to do but don't because society tells us not to. We are afraid for these young people—these girls—because the poor little things are alone and unprotected, but deep down we also recognise that we are afraid of them. Because out there in the woods we can no longer control them. It is this liminal space between protection and control in which Rose's play wields its greatest power.

Children and young people are not immune to the greater movements of society, they are not apart from society. The attempt to 'protect' them seems more like a means of reinforcing the status quo, in which everyone wakes up tomorrow happy that things will be pretty much the same as yesterday. But there is a pivotal point of adolescent development, where young people realise that there is no clearly defined 'right and wrong', that the systems that give us safety also oppress us, that alternative ideas, while dangerous, also hold merit, and that sometimes it is the conflict between these two ideas of what their future can be that drives social change, for better or worse. Children know that change is inevitable and preferable to stagnation, otherwise they will be 'little' forever.

The conflicts between social conformity and individual freedom, between rules and desires, tradition and evolution, young and old, right and wrong, all create change but more importantly for us, create drama.

This is not a new concept. *little girls alone in the woods* was based on an exploration of Euripides' *The Bacchae* and, as such, addresses some of the same themes and issues of that play. Euripides himself, from the information we know or can extrapolate, was a subversive. Of all the Ancient Greek playwrights, his plays were among the few remaining that did not win any prizes in the bi-annual play competitions of Athens. Euripides' works promoted anti-war sentiment (evidenced in *The Trojan Women* and *Hecuba*) and the power of women in society (*Medea*, *Iphegenia in Taurus* and *The Orestia*). He was unpopular due to his intellectualism and subversion of the dominant Athenian paradigm that war is glorious, women are property, and that theatre is a place to purge pity and fear (*catharsis*) and not a place to make social comment.

The Bacchae was Euripides' warning to Athenian society that to ignore the power of the gods or nature, in favour of the seeming safety and order of civilisation, was to ignore the balance between humans and that greater power of which they were at the mercy.

The German philosopher Friedrich Nietzsche, in his book *The Birth of Tragedy*, discusses the Ancient Greek concept of the *dichotomy*[1] between the Apollonian and Dionysian. At one end of the scale is Apollo: the god of civilisation, logic, maths, order and music. At the other is the wild abandonment of Dionysus: god of wine, nature, impulse, chaos and theatre. Both are in a constantly changing balance of power. Nietzsche argues that too much Apollonian influence leads to a dry, controlled, stagnant society, while too much of the Dionysian influence results in a society focused on immediate desires, creativity without focus or purpose, and abandonment of 'civilised' or socially conscious behaviour. Therefore, there is a constantly changing conversation between the two that never stops moving one way or the other. If there ever was a balance, it could only be momentary or else the opposing forces would render society stagnate. Each needs the other to survive.

In *The Bacchae*, Euripides followed the structure of a tragedy as outlined by Aristotle in his *Poetics*. King Pentheus, a hero (someone

---

[1] *dichotomy |dī'kädəmē| noun (plural dichotomies) [usually in singular]*
a division or contrast between two things that are or are represented as being opposed or entirely different: a rigid dichotomy between science and mysticism.• Botany repeated branching into two equal parts. (https://www. lexico.com/definition/dichotomy)

of greater social or moral standing), is faced with a *dilemma* (all the women are leaving for an alternative society in the woods). Because of his fatal flaw (*hubris*) of excessive pride in his own laws and rule, he makes an error of judgement (*hamartia*) in saying Dionysus is not a god. Dionysus seduces Pentheus into wearing drag and visiting the female community, where he comes to the realisation (*anagnoresis*) that his laws are a hollow construct. The understanding (*apotheosis*) that there must be constant negotiation between the two powers is gruesomely shown by Pentheus' death, dismemberment and display by a key member of the group of women—his own mother.

If not for Pentheus trying to impose order and control over something natural and therefore within the mandate of the gods, the tragic outcome would not eventuate. If Pentheus had not seen the Bacchae as a threat to his own order and control of society, he would not have pit the Apollonian social order and control (i.e. man-made law) against the personification of the Dionysian, the god himself, whom Pentheus the rationalist refuses to acknowledge as a god. He would not have engaged in a *dialectic*[2] with the god and been lured to his own death at the hands of those who he trusted to be more logical.

But what if we stepped back from these monumental forces of society, represented by kings, queens, heroes and gods? What if you're not in a position of power from which to fall and, like an ant watching a battle in the skies, you are merely forced to deal with the repercussions of someone else's fight?

This is exactly what Rose has done with *little girls alone in the woods*.

Caught between oppositional forces, which seem too monumental for the disempowered youth to make a difference, Rose's characters are forced to exist between the known and the aspirational—the known society that they have been taught, full of rules and expectations but

---

2 *dialectic* |ˌdīə'lektik| *Philosophy noun (also dialectics) [usually treated as singular] 1 the art of investigating or discussing the truth of opinions.2 inquiry into metaphysical contradictions and their solutions.• the existence or action of opposing social forces, concepts, etc. The ancient Greeks used the term dialectic to refer to various methods of reasoning and discussion in order to discover the truth. (New Oxford American Dictionary)*

with the comfort and familiarity of clearly defined limitations, and the unknown, idealistic and full of promise and change but with no guarantee.

The contemporary relevance is obvious. Rallying against traditional views on environmental issues, racial discrimination and sexuality are all things that young people are trying to reconcile with the understanding that individual freedom versus social responsibility is not a one-or-the-other, binary argument.

This play is a tragedy told from the point of view of the victims, of the powerless, the bystanders and underdogs of society, whether that be youth, women, or LGBTQI people. This play explores the little people and the effect that the greater powers have upon them.

The perspective allows us to see greater global influences and shifts through the eyes of the disempowered. These massive changes are happening around them, clashing and arguing their points and leaving the 'everyday' person to decide what it means to them. What is more important to the individual? Large scale social unrest, or the fact that they have an assignment due tomorrow? Because, try as they might, the system still dictates what their immediate responsibilities are. Rules and personal freedom, school and life, friends and self, creativity or rationalism – name your dichotomy.

Regardless of their individual motivations, what we see is young people and their ideas and actions invalidated by the pressure to conform to social norms, consumerism, and the erosion of civil liberties, all in favour of 'protection'. The different, the divergent thinkers, the subversives, the creative thinkers and artists, whose contributions to society are not quantitative, are seen as undermining the status-quo and are therefore to be feared, banished and restricted.

Within this script, Rose has given an authentic voice to those who we barely hear. The five 'Townies'—representations of the dedicated student, the aggressive feminist, the right-wing voice of popular opinion, the voice of popular youth opinion, the floppy-haired boy writing poetry and the kid who is just trying to get through life—help put the story in perspective.

The relationships between the characters explore the themes beautifully as they argue their own points of view or opinions, but more than that, their imaginations provide the quality of what is not seen in the play. They imagine and project an attitude and behaviours towards these 'wild women' in the woods without any basis in fact and, because there is no other information beyond gossip, they believe this to be truth, rather than the smoke-screen of popular opinion. This is like the concept of *yugen*[3] in Japanese art where a painting of a mountain is obscured by cloud, asking the viewer to enter into and engage with the art enough to fill in the hidden sections with their own imagination.

In *little girls ...*, the role of the chorus is integral, as it is in all Ancient Greek plays. They set the tone, they comment on the ideas, they relate to the lead characters—in this piece, far greater than in the classics. The chorus not only represent the ideal or perceived perspective of the Townies, but also provide the stark reality of the true situation once they are given the voice to do so through their interaction with the character of Alina. The chorus are both the perceived expectation and the reality.

The girls left the known safety of society, and the protective armour of their parents, to seek out a place where they could be extreme, passionate, creative and more in tune with the beauty of nature. They, like the Bacchae, are free women, not mindless followers. Brave enough to shed their constructed identity as young people, and young women in particular, this chorus consists of women willing to challenge the social ideal of power, gender, purpose, beauty and art.

The townies see them as wild and free, somewhat irresponsible, but taking a risk to pursue an alternative to the dominant paradigm. They are regarded with scorn, and yet some admiration, for standing up to their given situation and abandoning the safety of societal norms for the chance at something more liberating.

Is Dionysus real, or is he merely a symbol of the alternate perspective? In our first production of the play, we argued that question for hours and finally decided that it didn't matter. Dionysus becomes real for Alina and the rest of the girls because they deify a feeling and an idea and, as

---

[3] *yugen (yoo-gen) the mystery of the universe. That which is beyond sight, but alludes to a greater existence. 'When looking at autumn mountains through mist, the view may be indistinct yet have great depth. Although few autumn leaves may be visible through the mist, the view is alluring. The limitless vista created in imagination far surpasses anything one can see more clearly.' (Kamo no Chōmei in Hume, 253–54)*

a result, they feel the need to act as prophets of this concept and share their discoveries with the town. Before they can explain, however, the town's attempts to 'protect the innocent' stop the possibility of growth in its tracks, eventually bringing ruin unto the town itself. A poignant tragedy.

In that regard, isn't it interesting to consider why it is that only women abandon the town for the woods? Their femininity and their freedom are compromised so they boldly leave to find an alternative. The fact that they realise the Apollonian has just as many benefits and issues as the Dionysian doesn't undermine these women, but grounds them in a society where they know and are able to articulate inconsistencies and prejudice.

The messenger roles are a brilliant choice to provide the common voice of young people in relating what they see and think, both in the reporting of the 'craze' as well as in the final aftermath. These are people who feel connected to and invested in in the events, simply because of their age and circumstance and because they are ere there as part of the moment. The messengers may not involve themselves in the action, or understand how it comes about, but they witness it from their own perspectives and report it from that same perspective. In this respect, they are the audience who experience more in life through second hand reportage than personal involvement.

It is clear that one of the themes in the play is how to manage the allure of freedom with its wild, creative and chaotic possibilities. The characters know the rules, but they also see the benefit of going beyond them. Through their rebellion, they decide which rules to follow and which to push.

Teenagers' need to assert their individuality is essentially their first foray into the Dionysian—rebellion, perceived freedom—and despite their understanding of how the Apollonian rules can help them in this society, they also long for the ability to let go and abandon themselves to new experiences and understandings. It is one of the dominant tensions that teenagers feel and stereotypically rebel against and it is this constant rebalancing that leads to a greater understanding of their own truth.

As the German philosopher Immanuel Kant postured, thesis versus antithesis leads to synthesis. In this case the rules of society act as the thesis; the desire for something better, different and free becomes the antithesis; and the conversation between them becomes something new—a synthesis.

These young people live in their society, are a product of it and also the engineers of its evolution. Trying to 'protect' the children, or removing them from their own context and society, enforcing old rules and beliefs, would leave them out of place and time.

little girls alone in the woods challenges the validity of a youth perspective and shows that it is as worthy as any other, accepting all that could influence it. It is an authentic, relevant voice that resonates with young people and asks older generations to consider their relationship with them. At the whim of these social, 'god-like' forces, the disempowered youth can only react, but by doing so, they realise there are alternate choices, broadening their awareness and initiating social change.

They realise that:

You can't trust anything, but you can trust everything.

Perception and perspective are not the same.

Dichotomy doesn't mean black or white; it is a conversation between them.

You are as much a product of your society as you are a part of it.

Most importantly, it shows that sometimes being *alone* in the woods is a necessary part of our lives.

Simon Tate

Simon Tate is a teacher, writer, director and facilitator of performance for young people in secondary and tertiary education and the theatre industry in Brisbane. He commissioned *little girls alone in the woods* for the Queensland Academy Creative Industries Campus and was privileged to direct its first production in 2017. He's just some guy who knows some stuff.

for Tatey:
his ideas,
his revolt

little girls alone in the woods was first produced as *The Howl* at Queensland Academy of Creative Industries, Brisbane, on 2 November 2017 with the following cast:

ALINA	Indiah Morris
CLEO	Amy Lehman
LUCKY	Ava Keogan
ELLE	Josephine Hawley
REX	William Kaspar
DYLAN	Levi Grayson-Riley
TODD	Vincent D'Amico
MESSENGER 1	Nim Dewhurst
MESSENGER 2	Penny Shekarian
MESSENGER 3	Bryce Delaney
THE BACCHAE	Aniella Bacquiran, Ella Boon, Micol Carmagni, Zoe Hill, Vedika Karayil, Bonnie Morrow, Susan Salisbury, Maggie Solomon, Lois Sutcliffe, Roison Wallace Nash, Keely Woods

Directors, Simon Tate and Katie Fletcher
Stage Manager, Maddy Macrae
Assistant Stage Managers, Maddie Prebble and Matilda Knight
Stage Crew, Claudia Stringer, Elysha McIntyre, Lagvu Jhala and Genna Garvey
Lighting Designer, Michael Richardson
Lighting Operator, Vrinda Eswaran
Set Construction, Lois Sutcliffe and Nim Dewhurst
Sound, Will Kaspar and Aniella Bacquiran
AV, Vincent D'Amico, Bryce Delaney and Indiah Morris
Costumes, Penny Shekarian, Maggie Solomon, Chloe Wang, Jacqueline Coelho, Molly Glanville, Bella Abraham, Chris Perlinski and Ethan Tran
Hair and Makeup, Mary-Helen Buchan and Jessica Duncliffe

The cast of the 2017 Queensland Academy of Creative Industries production in Brisbane. (Photo: Craig English)

CHARACTERS

The Kids:

A group of teenagers who all go to the same school. They have an informal study group after school.

LUCKY, can be any gender (change pronouns accordingly), currently on the cusp of failing three classes

DYLAN, male, a wannabe Instagram star

ROB, male, depressive and poetic, loves a good cry

REX, male, his father is on the police force and his upbringing has been strict

ALINA, female, reliable, hard worker, the one everyone counts on

CLEO, female, doesn't really give a shit, does the bare minimum to get by and it works

ELLE, female, quiet and studious, people often ask her for help with their school work

MESSENGER 1, can be any gender, goes to school with the kids, but isn't really in their group

MESSENGER 2, can be any gender, homeschooled, potentially a bit younger than everyone else, lives across the street from the bush

MESSENGER 3, can be any gender, sibling of Messenger 2

VIOLET, the first to leave.

The Bacchae:

A group of young women who have disappeared into the bush.

The number of Bacchae is very flexible. Anywhere from 5–50 performers may be used.

SETTING

A town somewhere.

The bush on the outskirts of that town.

The border between the bush and the town.

NOTES

On Mode of Address:

All characters are aware of the audience at all times. They know they are characters in a play. They move between speaking to the audience and other characters without a shift in style.

On Choral Text:

The Bacchae often speak in chorus. Text indented and indicated [*in chorus*] is choral. Text assigned to the Bacchae that is not indented and indicated as chorus may be either solo or choral, at the discretion of the director.

Other:

A slash (/) indicates overlapping text. The following line should begin at the point of the slash.

ONE: PROLOGUE

VIOLET *enters. She is a young girl. A busker. She sets up. This can take a while.*

A moment. She looks out at the audience.

She begins to perform.

The song is about to swell, she is about to hit the emotional high note when a computerised voice interrupts—

VOICE: What is your name?

    She stops.

VIOLET: Sorry?

VOICE: What is your name?

VIOLET: Um. Violet.

VOICE: Age?

VIOLET: Sixteen.

VOICE: Gender?

VIOLET: Why?

VOICE: Please produce your permit.

VIOLET: What?

VOICE: Is a legal guardian present at this time to supervise your safety?

VIOLET: Um … no.

VOICE: Have your legal guardians filed Form 780: Permit for a Minor to Perform Creative Content Without Supervision by a Legal Guardian, including Appendix A: Risk Assessment, and Appendix B: Family Tree, and paid the application processing fee?

VIOLET: I don't know.

VOICE: After filing, Form 780 takes four to eight weeks to process and you may resume activity at that time.

VIOLET: It's a really short song, can I just—?

VOICE: Goodbye.

    VIOLET *stands for a moment. She is upset. Slowly the upset turns to anger and the anger turns to resolve.*

    She whispers the following line, but it is amplified, and echoes through the theatre:

VIOLET: Dionysus.

TWO: EPISODE 1

The KIDS *sit amongst piles and piles of books. They alternate between reading/writing/typing and staring out at the audience.*

REX: It's important to try to go on like everything is normal.
DYLAN: Even when things aren't.
CLEO: At least that's what they say.
ROB: It's important to move forward with everyday activities.
DYLAN: That essay on *Animal Farm* isn't going anywhere.
ALINA: The trick is getting your brain to listen. To stop it from just.
CLEO: From just wandering.
DYLAN: Just stop thinking. About just. Everything.
ALINA: Stop. Thinking. And do the thing.
CLEO: Just do the thing.
ALINA: Stop thinking.
REX: Yeah.
ALINA: I'm trying not to think about awful things. All the awful things.
CLEO: Impending terror. A variety of doom.
LUCKY: I'm trying not to think about how I could really go for a cheeseburger right now but maybe I shouldn't because, you know, *reasons*, but god, how / good are cheeseburgers?
DYLAN: I'm trying not to think about how I'm eight hours and fifteen minutes in sleep debt and forests turned / to soot.
ROB: I'm trying not to think about children sewing buttons onto my shirt.
CLEO: I'm trying not to think about how these jeans are so tight it hurts to sit down, but it's / worth it.
ALINA: I'm trying not to think about little girls disappearing into darkness.
DYLAN: I'm trying not think about how I want to start a veggie patch, but my dad said it's too expensive to water it every day, and it's cheaper to just buy the veggies from / Coles.
ALINA: I'm trying not think about Dionysus.
LUCKY: What?

     ALINA *has surprised and confused herself.*

ALINA: I don't really know what I mean by that.
CLEO: Oh my god, I'm never wearing these again, I can't breathe.

ROB: Maybe I'll learn to sew and start making my own clothes.

DYLAN: That's so expensive.

LUCKY: And time consuming.

ALINA: I'm trying not think about—

LUCKY: Sorry, I have to finish / this.

REX: I'm just. I'm focussing on Pablo Picasso. Pablo. Picasso.

ALINA: I'm trying not to think about all the awful things that have been happening.
>The stillness
>in / the air.

DYLAN: My mum is worried.

CLEO: Lots of people are / worried.

REX: Pablo Picasso was once suspected of having stolen the Mona Lisa. He was questioned by the police. Did you know that?

> *No answer.*

>I have an essay due / on Friday.

CLEO: Lots of people are worried.

DYLAN: But we're just going on like normal.

ROB: Because we have to.

CLEO: Like normal,
>but / worried.

ALINA: Like normal,
>but waiting
>for things to get worse.

DYLAN: Continuing until we can't continue.

ROB: Like normal,
>but with a low buzz

CLEO: in the background.

ROB: Like normal but with a quicker / pulse.

DYLAN: A slight / fever.

ROB: A dry heat, a static / electric

CLEO: residue of a night / terror

DYLAN: or a plane circling.

ROB: Like politicians with furrowed brows and calm voices.

CLEO: We're all thinking about all the awful things that have been happening.
>But things / are—

LUCKY: I have a test
    tomorrow
    in Advanced Algebra.
CLEO: But things / are—
LUCKY: And I'm going to fail it.
CLEO: But things are just the same. Despite.
DYLAN: Despite everything that's happened.
REX: I'm going to start with a summary of Cubism, which, we know was
    an important movement that eventually brought us Modern Art.
CLEO: [*dripping with sarcasm*] Fascinating! Tell us more about Cubism,
    Rex!
REX: Basically what it is, Cubism, is instead of a painting from like
    one point of view, the artist would like show a thing, an object from
    multiple viewpoints but all at once.
        That's all I've got so far.
CLEO: He was also a misogynist.
REX: What?
CLEO: Picasso. Big misogynist.
REX: Um. Well. That's not, not in this book. Or the Wikipedia article.
LUCKY: Wait. We can use Wikipedia as a source?
REX: No! God no! I'm just using it for an overview.
CLEO: Seriously, tons of his girlfriends literally killed themselves.
REX: Because of him?
CLEO: Probs. All those old famous artists were assholes. They were like
    the Woody Allens of their time.
REX: I mean, this is supposed to be an essay on Picasso's influence on
    the future of art, so I just … don't know if I should put the misogy-
    nist stuff in …
ALINA: So we all have a presentation to give tomorrow on our five-year
    plan. I've been practising my presentation in front of Pearl. Pearl's
    my pet rabbit. She's very supportive. It's a large portion of our mark,
    but I'm not worried, because I've put in the work. And that's a good
    feeling. It's the best feeling, actually. The satisfaction of knowing
    you did the work. Like … there's nothing better.
CLEO: What about a really good meal?
ALINA: But a good meal, you feel fat after.
CLEO: Yeah, but what about like a really good healthy meal?

ALINA: Maybe a good healthy meal, but even so there are things to consider. Where did the ingredients come from? Is your enjoyment of that meal contributing to the suffering of anyone?

CLEO: I mean. Yeah. Probably.

ALINA: My presentation of my five-year plan hasn't hurt anyone. Except maybe myself. Being stuck in my room. Working. Instead of outside playing.

LUCKY: Outside *playing?*

ALINA: Okay, instead of sitting on my bed for three hours watching YouTube.

CLEO: Yeah.

ALINA: But it's worth it.

CLEO: Sure. Whatever.

DYLAN: My five-year plan is to crack 100,000 followers.

CLEO: That's a terrible plan.

DYLAN: It's not. You can earn over a thousand dollars a post if you are perceived to have a loyal following.

CLEO: My plan is to buy lots of lotto tickets.

LUCKY: Did anyone do the Maths homework yet?

CLEO: Nah.

REX: Yeah.

LUCKY: What did you get for number 18?

REX: x equals 5.

LUCKY: Oh no.

REX: What?

LUCKY: I got x equals 142.

REX: What?

ROB: 142?

CLEO: One of you is wrong.

REX: [*with sarcasm*] Oh, really? One of us is wrong?

LUCKY: Where's Elle? She said she would help me.

CLEO: Haven't heard from her.

DYLAN: That's weird. She's like annoyingly punctual.

LUCKY: Well, has anyone else done it?

ROB: No, I'm just finishing up my five-year plan and then I'll start on the Maths.

LUCKY: Wait, when is the five-year plan due?

ROB: Tomorrow.

LUCKY: Oh my god. Oh my god. I completely forgot about that. When am I going to …? Oh my god.

DYLAN: Um. Tonight?

LUCKY: I think I'm going to have a panic attack.

ROB: Do you want a plastic bag?

He holds out a plastic bag.

ALINA: A paper bag, you idiot. A plastic bag would just suffocate them.

ROB: Well … I don't have a paper bag.

LUCKY: Seriously, where is Elle? I have no idea what I'm doing.

CLEO: You don't think she …

LUCKY: What?

ALINA: Is in the bush.

LUCKY: What are you talking about?

ALINA: Uh. Those girls?

LUCKY stares blankly.

The girls who ran away to the bush?

LUCKY: What girls?

CLEO: How can you not know this?

ALINA: Seriously, it's everywhere.

ROB: It literally is.

LUCKY: I don't know. I've been a little stressed. And my dad took away my phone.

DYLAN: Oh my god, why?

LUCKY: He said I was an addict.

DYLAN: That's not okay.

LUCKY: Well, I sort of am. Now I have this.

It's an old-school flip phone.

CLEO: Cool.

DYLAN: Jesus, what's the point of that?

LUCKY: I know. Anyway. What happened?

DYLAN: So there's like eight girls in town they can't find.

REX: Eleven.

CLEO: No, there's only like eight.

REX: No. There's eleven.

CLEO: Pretty sure that's an exaggeration.

REX: My father works for the police department, and he's seen all the reports and there are definitely eleven and more leaving all the time.

LUCKY: What are you talking about? Where are they going?

DYLAN: They think they're just like off in the bush.

LUCKY: Like. Dead?

CLEO: No. Fully alive.

ROB: They are just living it up in the bush like a bunch of wild lesbians.

CLEO: They aren't lesbians.

ROB: They might be lesbians.

CLEO: That's just your weird male fear of women hanging out in spaces without men present talking.

ROB: No, seriously, some of them could be lesbians.

CLEO: Yes. True. Some of them could be lesbians, but there is no logic in labelling the entire group of women as lesbians. You're just scared of not being needed and your only other experience of that is with lesbians so you're projecting your fear onto this group of women whose sexual orientation we know nothing about.

DYLAN: Harsh.

REX: So. Where's Elle?

LUCKY: I don't know.

CLEO: It's pretty weird.

ALINA: No way. She's not the type to. She loves …

DYLAN: What?

ALINA: Civilisation.

REX: Who doesn't love civilisation? Look at us! What do we have to complain about?

LUCKY: This stupid assignment.

REX: Exactly. The extent of our complaints is Maths.

CLEO: And you know …

REX: What?

CLEO: Well. Racism, sexism, human trafficking, coral bleaching, global warming, internet trolls, factory farms—

REX: Okay okay. We get it.

CLEO: But *do* you?

ROB: So you think Elle …

LUCKY: Maybe she had a dentist's appointment.

DYLAN: Have you called her?

LUCKY: I don't have any numbers in this stupid phone. Can someone
  message her?
DYLAN: She's offline.
CLEO: What?
ALINA: Send it anyway.
DYLAN: Okay.

> *He texts.*

Sent.

> *They all sit in silence and stare at the phone.*

> *The phone dings.*

She's just getting coffee.

> *The phone dings again.*

She wants to know if any of you want anything.
LUCKY: I'll take a long black.

THREE: ODE 1

A fantasy inside the heads of powerful men.

VOICE: Please begin.

> *The* BACCHAE. *They are all wearing pastel pajamas. They have
> a pillow fight with bright pastel pillows. It's choreographed to
> music. It's beautiful and sweet: a classic Hollywood image of teen
> girls. Feathers float through the air like snow.*

> *But ...*

> *As the fight progresses, it begins to change. It becomes more and
> more violent and less and less beautiful.*

> *It's a nightmare.*

Stop.
Stop.
Stop!

> *Blackout.*

> *Loud classical music in the darkness.*

> *The music abruptly stops.*

FOUR: EPISODE 2

REX: Elle, you have to fill in this form.

ELLE: What?

REX: If you are female you have to fill one out. You can get them at the post office, but my dad gave me these ones for all of you. They need to be mailed back by Wednesday.

CLEO: What are they for?

REX: Registration.

ELLE: For what?

REX: Safety registration.

ELLE: I don't understand.

REX: It's like a database. So they know who you all are, and they can like keep track of you. 'Cause, you know. All the girls disappearing. They just want to like … make sure you are all okay.

ALINA: Seriously?

REX: It's for your own good.

CLEO: Sure it is.

ELLE: Give it here. Let's get this over with.

Keely Woods, Issy Salisbury and Mary-Helen Buchan in the 2017 Queensland Academy of Creative Industries production in Brisbane. (Photo: Craig English)

ALINA *gives a frustrated scream.*

REX: What?

ALINA: I wanna like, like ... break a pencil. Arrrhhhh!

CLEO: Whoa. New levels of rage from Alina. Hide your office supplies, everyone.

REX: Why is she raging?

ALINA: Like they are all off partying in the bush and we're stuck here filling in forms.

ELLE: Yeah, agreed, I really don't have time for this.

REX: It should only take about seven minutes. See, it says at the top—

ALINA: Like who's gonna help with our group biology project? Or play the flute solo in youth orchestra?! What, we're just supposed to skip the flute solo?! Hello?! It's *printed* in the *score* written by *Mozart* like a *million* years ago. I mean, yes, we are *all* upset about *something*. And *yes* we *all* want to run away because we *all* think there are more important things in life than Mozart but. Like. We have to do what we have to do. And right now we have to do *Mozart*. You know?

Everyone is staring at ALINA. *A pause.*

CLEO: I mean. Do we? Do we have to do Mozart?

REX: No, yeah. I totally agree. It needs to stop. The forms are only the first step.

ELLE: What do you mean?

REX: Oh. My dad said they are gonna put up a fence around the perimeter of the town.

ELLE: Who?

REX: Like. The city.

CLEO: Wow.

REX: Yeah. He said they are getting like five hundred phone calls a day about it all. And they still have no idea why it's happening or how to stop it.

ALINA: Argh! It's so *selfish*! I just think they are being so *selfish*!

Everyone is staring at her again.

I'm sorry. That was an overreaction.

Um. Just. Maddie, she plays flute in youth orchestra with me, and she disappeared last week and I just ...

I'm fine. Never mind, I'm fine.

Long pause.

DYLAN: Do you know my older sister Hannah?

ELLE: Yeah.

DYLAN: Well, her best friend Kaya disappeared

ROB: It just keeps happening …

DYLAN: Yeah. She disappeared yesterday. Here, I'll show you a photo. She was really pretty.

ELLE: Is.

DYLAN: What?

ELLE: She *is* really pretty. She's not dead.

CLEO: As far as we know. Also pretty by whose standards?

DYLAN: Mine.

LUCKY: It happened to this girl from the other soccer team we played last Friday.

CLEO: Shit.

LUCKY: We beat them.

CLEO: Good job.

LUCKY: I think they were all kinda disturbed by it, so they were easy to beat.

ROB: It happened to the granddaughter of this guy my mum works with.

LUCKY: I also thought it happened to this girl in my Chem class but she just had food poisoning.

DYLAN: Well, Kaya's parents saw her leaving the house at like eleven p.m. in her pajamas, and they were all, 'Kaya where are you going?' and she didn't say anything and she just kept walking and that was the last time they saw her.

LUCKY: Yeah, apparently the soccer girl just left in the middle of dinner. Same thing. Like didn't say anything. Just got up and walked off.

ELLE: Sounds like a disease. Like a brain disease.

ROB: Like zombies. Like they are all turning to zombies

REX: And it could happen to anyone. At any time.

CLEO: Well.

REX: What?

CLEO: Like it's not gonna happen to you. You're a dude.

REX: Well … no.

CLEO: But it could happen to me.

REX: Maybe. I hope not. I mean. You're too smart for that.

CLEO: Who knows?

REX: What?

LUCKY: Does anyone know when the sonnet analysis is due?

ALINA: Tomorrow.

LUCKY: Shit.

CLEO: Sounds kinda nice, doesn't it?

ELLE: What?

CLEO: Running away to the bush.

ALINA: Jesus, don't say that.

A nervous laugh from REX.

CLEO: I think I'd be okay with it.

ALINA: Shut up.

CLEO: Possessed by the spirit of the trees.

REX: Um.

CLEO: Walking in a trance into the sunset.

ALINA: Stop it.

CLEO: Why?

ALINA: They aren't in a trance. They aren't zombies.

CLEO: What do you mean?

ALINA: They are like … eyes wide open, running off to do whatever the hell they want in the bush.

REX: Yeah. And that's how they're gonna die. It's the dumbest thing they've ever done.

DYLAN: Maybe they are being hypnotised.

ALINA: No way. They want it.

CLEO: How do you know?

ALINA: Who wouldn't want that?

DYLAN: I wouldn't. There are no toilets in the bush.

ELLE: Oh my god, don't be pathetic.

DYLAN: I'm not being pathetic. Have you *been* camping?

ELLE: Not really.

DYLAN: I go with my parents every summer and you're just sticky and dirty and like thirsty for a week. And sleeping is uncomfortable. And you have to shit in a hole.

CLEO: Ugh.

DYLAN: Yeah. You shit in a hole and you bury it.

REX: What about the toilet paper?

DYLAN: You bury that too.

ROB: Gross.

LUCKY: So with the sonnet, is it one page?

ELLE: Four pages.

LUCKY: Shit.

ELLE: What do you think they're doing out there?

ROB: I think they're being all witchy. And they're casting spells on us. Like summoning spirits and brewing potions.

CLEO: Oh my god, yes. They're like chanting and making little charms out of sticks to curse us all. And they're walking on water and levitating.

DYLAN: I think one of them has a big mansion somewhere in the middle of the bush and they are there dancing to Kanye and drinking champagne. And famous people have like heard about it and are trying to find it but it's so exclusive they are turning them away. And they are popping pills and wearing designer clothes and lounging around in swimming pools eating junk food.

CLEO: No way. It's just a big hippie orgy.

ALINA: I don't really care what they are doing, because they clearly don't care what we are doing.

LUCKY: I think it's just quiet. And all you can hear is the wind and the birds. And they are just enjoying not being able to hear traffic. And they are sleeping for like fourteen hours a day. And then waking up and braiding each other's hair and then going back to sleep in the quiet.

CLEO: That's nice, Lucky. That's a nice thought.

LUCKY: Thanks.

CLEO: But honestly, they are probably taking hallucinogens and doing yoga.

ROB: Maybe they are just going back, back to how it was before. And they are learning how to survive. And they are building fires. And making houses out of sticks and mud—

ELLE: Or it's utopia. They've made a perfect society. Where everyone wears white and sways together in prayer in the morning, and it's just like gentle love and happiness all the time.

REX: I heard they are killing animals.

CLEO: What?

ALINA: No they're not.

REX: Yeah they are. That's what my dad says. They believe you make a sacrificial offering and then you perform this ritual that sends you into a state where you basically become a wild animal living in the bush.

CLEO: You're so paranoid.

REX: I'm not paranoid.

CLEO: Sacrificial offerings? Why do you have to make everything negative and like a conspiracy theory?

REX: How is this not a conspiracy? Girls are disappearing into the—

ALINA *abruptly stands up. Everyone looks at her.*

ALINA: I have to—

Pause.

ELLE: What?

ALINA: I don't know.

ALINA *walks off without a word.*

REX: Where is she going?

CLEO: I don't know.

LUCKY: Maybe the toilet?

FIVE: ODE 2

The BACCHAE. *A heap of mangled bodies, and pillows—as if the pillow fight had been a war.*

VOICE: Clean up.

A moment.

Then the girls begin to get up—slowly.

They take the pillowcases off the pillows. We think they are cleaning up the place. But instead, they put the pillowcases on their heads like balaclavas.

They stand with pillowcase-balaclavas on their heads, staring at the audience.

A moment.

Clean up.

They stand.

Clean up!

BACCHAE: Quiet.

> *The* BACCHAE *speak to the audience.*

>> [*In chorus*] It wasn't one thing.
>> It wasn't even a collection of things.
>> It was just a persistent discomfort.
>> Like a blanket over your face on a hot night.
>> I wanted it off.
>> Off my face.

>> What happened was—
>> Well—
>> Okay, so like,
>> I had been feeling—
>> I mean I've always felt—
>> I didn't realise it, but I've always felt like—
>> Sorry, it's hard to explain.

What happened was
my grandfather came over for dinner
and asked me
again
if I had a boyfriend.
I said, 'No'.
He said,
'You'll find someone eventually.
You're a beautiful girl.'
And I felt sad.
For so many reasons.
The blanket
over my face
while I sat
at dinner
eating steamed carrots, quietly
petrified
that I will never be enough.

What happened was
Andrew,

this guy I know,
we were in the food court
at the shopping centre
after seeing a movie,
it was a date,
and he grabbed my hand,
and stared at me
like,
aggressively,
with this fake-sincere look,
and said,
'You have beautiful eyes'.
And I felt really sorry for him
because
he thought
that sentence
would unlock me.
That all I needed to hear
to love him
for eternity
was that my eyes were beautiful.
And I wished I could close my eyes forever
so he couldn't look at them.

What happened was
I said to the doctor,
'It hurts'.
He nodded
and sent me home.

What happened was
I followed the rules
wore the clothes
thought the thoughts
and they called me sweet
and shook their heads.
I stopped following the rules
but their heads were still shaking.

Every word I say
is candy coated and swallowed.

But I'm not sweet.
I'm serious.

> [*In chorus*] Maybe if I was older.
> Maybe if I was larger.
> Or smaller,
> or prettier,
> or uglier,
> or gruffer.
> Maybe if I was something else
> I would feel like
> I existed.
> Like I could say something
> and people would turn their heads
> because they heard it
> and believed it.

What happened was
it was a Friday.
I had no plans.
I was bored. Things felt wrong.

And
like lightning
magic relief
from the grey of no contact
the ding of a message.
This girl.
She just moved here,
she's in the grade above me.
Heather.
She messaged me.
And she asked me if I wanted to come over
and stay the night
and watch Netflix
and stuff.

And I thought,
'Definitely'.

> [*In chorus*] So I did.
> And then in the middle of an episode of [*name of television show*]
> Heather said that her older brother
> (he's like twenty-two)
> and his friends were all gonna go hang out in the car park by the water
> and we should definitely go.
> She said her mum wouldn't let us, but we could sneak out after she went to bed.
>
> I knew it was probably a bad idea.
> And it didn't even sound that fun to me.
> But I said okay.

We took pillows and made bodies in the sheets.
I thought they looked pretty realistic.
We climbed out the window,
we walked to the water.
It was further than I thought.
And when we got there
this group of people were standing around all these old televisions
and they were smashing them
with a baseball bat.
And they had beers
but I didn't drink any
because beer tastes disgusting.
One of them held out the bat.
I thought,
'Why are we smashing TVs?'
I said, 'What's the point of this?'
And Heather said, 'What's the point of anything?'
And I thought …
'Whoa'.
I took the bat.
And someone shouted,

'Fuck the system!'
I don't think they really meant it.
I think they just wanted to shout something.
But I felt something deep inside me jump.
I gripped the bat
hard
and I beat that television
into dust.
It was.
The greatest moment.
Of my life.
I screamed at the top of my lungs
and everyone stared at me.
But I didn't care.

Then a car came shooting towards us.
It was the police.
And they made us get in the back of the car.
They drove us back to Heather's.
Her mum had found the pillows.
Apparently, they weren't all that realistic.
I had to call my parents
but no-one answered.
'Cause they trust me.
'Cause I'd never done anything like that before.
So I left a voicemail.
And tried to sleep.
Knowing I was going to literally die in the morning.
My parents were going to literally kill me.
Not literally.
You know what I mean.
        [*In chorus*] Stop pretending you don't know what I mean.
I couldn't.
I couldn't sleep.
It was early morning.
Five a.m.
Or something.

Everything was still.
Heather was asleep.
She looked so peaceful.
She looked like a god.
And the sky was fragile.
It felt like this might be the last quiet moment of my life.
I looked down and my hand was bleeding.
There was
a little
piece of glass
a shard of television screen
in my finger
and I picked at it,
I squeezed it,
but I couldn't get it out.
It was in me.
It was part of me.
Forever.
I felt it in my belly
a yearning.
It was the truth.
And it was burning
and burning
and burning
and burning.
I looked around the room.
White walls.
Dirty laundry.
Poster of the constellations.
And I couldn't pretend anymore.
The whole world
was in trouble.

I stared at the sliver of glass
and it said,
'You think you are trapped, but you're not'.
And it said, 'Listen.
Listen close.

Are you listening?
>[*In chorus*] My name is Dionysus.
>We can make a new world.
>I will take you seriously.'

So I
slid open the window.
And slipped out.
Again.
And I walked.
For hours
through neighborhood streets
past chain stores downtown
along the freeway
through a dusty open plain
filled with gnats
that bit my face.
I walked into the bush
where the trees made it darker and colder.
I walked right into the river
until it rose over my shoulders.
It was freezing.
I was gasping.
>[*In chorus*] And I kept walking
>along the bottom of the river
>until I reached the other side
>and I emerged
>different.
>Ready. Waiting.
>For Dionysus
>to set me free.

>*Blackout.*

SIX: EPISODE 3

MESSENGER 1 *is standing facing the audience, trying to catch their breath. They are holding a tin of coconut milk.*

MESSENGER 1: I ran all the way here.

ROB: This is Alex.
MESSENGER 1: I just need to catch my breath.
ROB: Our parents are friends.
MESSENGER 1: I ran so fast. Oh my god.
CLEO: Why?
MESSENGER 1: Because I saw something.
LUCKY: Are you in my History class?
MESSENGER 1: No.
DYLAN: You're in the class below us, aren't you?
MESSENGER 1: Yeah. And I. And I saw something. That I. That I thought you'd wanna know about, Rob.
ROB: Okay.
ELLE: Tell us.
MESSENGER 1: What's on your ankle? Is that a glow stick?
REX: It's a tracking device. It's still in beta. I'm just testing it out for my dad.
ELLE: His dad works for the police.
MESSENGER 1: That's weird.
REX: I get two hundred dollars. And it's for a good cause. All females under eighteen years of age will be given one to wear as soon as testing is complete.
MESSENGER 1: I don't … know what to say …
CLEO: Ignore him.
REX: It's for safety!
ELLE: Right.
ROB: So tell us what happened!
MESSENGER 1: Okay. I was walking with Lester.
DYLAN: Who's Lester?
MESSENGER 1: Lester's my dog.
DYLAN: Cute. Do you have a photo?
CLEO: Ignore him too.
MESSENGER 1: Anyway, after school I was with Lester and we were going to Coles 'cause I was going to pick up some coconut milk 'cause Mum's making a curry. And I tied up Lester outside and I bought the coconut milk, and then when I came out Lester was like barking and barking at this girl who was like walking across the parking lot. And I was like, 'Oh my god, calm down', and then I looked, and it was Alina. And I like know how you feel about Alina.

ROB: Um. What? No.

MESSENGER 1: What? No, remember at your parents' barbecue when you told me—

ROB: That was like two years ago.

REX: So wait. You saw Alina today?

ELLE: Yeah, what? 'Cause she wasn't in school today.

LUCKY: She's sick. I think.

CLEO: She's clearly not sick if she's walking alone across the parking lot of Coles.

ROB: Can we just let him tell the freakin' story?

MESSENGER 1: Okay. So she had this weird look on her face. And she was holding an animal in her hands, like a little dog or something, and she had something red on her face—blood, oh god, let's face it, it was probably blood—and she was, she was walking towards the bush. You know where I mean?

ELLE: Yeah. Behind the Coles. The bush.

MESSENGER 1: Yeah, and I was all, 'Hey, Alina, where are you going?' 'Cause I kind of know her a little bit 'cause we are on the same bus route, you know? But she just looked at me and didn't say anything. I know she heard me though 'cause she definitely looked at me. But she just kept walking towards the bush. And I yelled at her like, 'You know you're not supposed to go in the bush!' 'Cause you know, she could get in a lot of trouble. But she just ignored me … and started climbing over the construction site for the fence thing they are building.

REX: What?!

ELLE: Yeah, that is really weird.

REX: That's against the law.

MESSENGER 1: But ummm … yeah … ummmm …

DYLAN: What?

MESSENGER 1: I … umm … I followed her.

ROB: You followed her.

MESSENGER 1: Yeah.

CLEO: Whoa.

MESSENGER 1: It was just … it seemed like something was … I don't know … she seemed weird. And I just wanted to like. Make sure everything was okay. So I just. Yeah. I followed her.

DYLAN: That is so intense.

ELLE: Yeah, the bush is super creepy.

MESSENGER 1: It was! It was so intense and so creepy! That's exactly how it felt! And I mean I don't want to sound crazy but it looked sort of like she was floating, like not walking, like she was floating. Like a ghost or something.

REX: What? Oh my god!

CLEO: You are so full of shit.

MESSENGER 1: No, I mean, turns out she wasn't, it turns out, she wasn't floating, she was just like walking, like on her legs, like on her feet, but for a second from a distance I thought she was floating, and it was just like freaky. That's all I'm saying.

Anyway, when I got past the construction site, I called out to her again and she stopped and looked back at me, and we just like stared at each other for like twenty seconds probably, and then she started running as fast as she could, away from me. And I was like … whoa … she's running off into the bush. This is happening. And I thought, 'I could be a hero'. And I imagined myself on TV all like, 'No, I'm not a hero, I just did what needed to be done. It was more instinct than anything.' And I thought I'm gonna follow her, I'm gonna rescue her from the bush. And she was going really fast, so I was like running from tree to tree and hiding behind them, it was like I was in a war movie or something except it was just me following Alina through the bush by the Coles. But she kept going, further and further, like way past the Coles, and at one point the wind started blowing really hard and it sounded like people whispering, and Lester had run off in a different direction and I was completely alone and I was thinking, how am I gonna find my way back, and I was starting to realise that this was probably the worst idea I'd ever had in my entire life, and that I was probably gonna die in the bush, that I was going to get lost and eaten by animals, and I was sweaty and anxious and I thought I should just stop, I should turn back now, but I was so lost I couldn't turn back 'cause I had no idea where I was so I just kept going. And it must have been like forty minutes of running, which thank god I play basketball 'cause otherwise I think I would have fainted, but finally she stopped in this clearing. And she looked up at the moon. And I hid in this bush and watched. And she took the little furry animal-thing in her hands and she rubbed her face against it. And then she whispered something to it, I couldn't hear what, 'cause I was really far away, and then she, she broke its little neck.

ELLE: What?

MESSENGER 1: Yeah.

ROB: That's not true.

MESSENGER 1: No, no it's true. I swear. I saw it. And then she started running again and eventually she got to a river. And on the banks of the river were all the other girls. There were like twenty of them. I didn't recognise anyone except this one girl, Violet, who I went to kindergarten with. But then Lester found me again, and he ran up to me and started barking like crazy and they all looked over at me and so I just took off. I ran away. And Lester seemed to know the way back so I was like following him and I was running and running and I ran all the way out of the woods and I just kept running through town and here I am.

Pause.

And that's what happened.

ELLE: Oh my god.

MESSENGER 1: Yeah.

REX: So. Wow. You saw them.

MESSENGER 1: Yeah.

DYLAN: You saw all the girls.

MESSENGER 1: Yeah.

DYLAN: Out in the bush.

MESSENGER 1: Yeah.

CLEO: What were they doing?

MESSENGER 1: They were just … um … like … sitting there.

ELLE: What do you mean?

MESSENGER 1: They were sitting around. In the woods.

DYLAN: What were they wearing?

MESSENGER 1: Just like. Normal clothes.

CLEO: So. They weren't having a drugged-out orgy?

MESSENGER 1: No.

CLEO: But did they look like they were maybe like recovering from hav-ing a drugged-out orgy?

MESSENGER 1: No.

DYLAN: But people said there's like a big mansion and helicopter pad somewhere nearby?

MESSENGER 1: Not that I saw.

CLEO: Yeah. And people said there were famous people there too.

MESSENGER 1: No. Definitely no famous people.

CLEO: Were they like singing songs and casting spells?

MESSENGER 1: Nope.

ELLE: Maybe they were silently casting spells.

MESSENGER 1: It didn't seem like it.

REX: So they were just …

MESSENGER 1: Hanging out.

LUCKY: Huh.

> *Pause. They all consider this.*

MESSENGER 1: So. Um. I have to bring this coconut milk to my mum.

> *They all look at* MESSENGER 1.

> *Blackout.*

SEVEN: ODE 3

A single person in a pillowcase-balaclava stands watching the BACCHAE. *The* BACCHAE *(sans balaclavas) are engaged in various activities: reading, napping, eating a muesli bar, setting up a tent, et cetera. The balaclava-clad person removes her hood. It's* ALINA. *She has blood on her face and she's holding a dead rabbit. She approaches the* BACCHAE *and kneels to present the rabbit. They stare at her for a moment.*

BACCHAE 1: What is that?

BACCHAE 2: It's a rat, please get it away.

ALINA: It's a rabbit.

BACCHAE 1: Why are you holding a bloody rabbit?

ALINA: It's dead. Her name was Pearl.

BACCHAE 2: I don't think you should be touching it.

ALINA: I sacrificed her.

BACCHAE 2: Oh my god.

BACCHAE 1: Why?

ALINA: It's an offering

BACCHAE 1: An offering?

ALINA: To you. To your cause. I want to be a part of it.

BACCHAE 1: Okay.

ALINA: So. Can I join you?

BACCHAE 3: Anyone can join us. We don't need your dead pet.

ALINA: Then. What do you need?

BACCHAE 3: Nothing. You're here. You've joined. It's official.

ALINA: Oh. I. Pearl. I …

BACCHAE 4: That's so sad.

BACCHAE 5: We could bury her. Have a little ceremony?

ALINA: Okay.

BACCHAE 5: I'll get someone to dig a hole.

BACCHAE 4: I'll do it.

> ALINA *sits down, sad, confused.*

> *A moment.*

BACCHAE 1: Sorry about your rabbit.

ALINA: Thanks.

> *Pause.*

Can I ask you something?

BACCHAE 1: Sure.

ALINA: What is Dionysus?

BACCHAE 1: Dionysus is an idea.

ALINA: What kind of idea?

BACCHAE 1: If people aren't listening to you, you don't need them.

BACCHAE 2: Run away and start over.

BACCHAE 5: We were sick of not being taken seriously.

BACCHAE 3: And of being told to do things we didn't want to do, and ignore things we didn't want to ignore.

ALINA: Me too.

BACCHAE 3: Then sit with us.

ALINA: I will!

BACCHAE 1: Welcome.

ALINA: [*with newfound resolve*] I would like to offer Pearl to Dionysus. As proof that I—

BACCHAE 1: No. That's not … No.

BACCHAE 2: Yeah. Stop.

ALINA: Sorry.

A moment.

So what do we do?

BACCHAE 5: What do you mean?

ALINA: What's next? What's the plan? What do we do?

BACCHAE 2: This is it.

BACCHAE 5: You're doing it.

ALINA: I don't understand.

BACCHAE 1: You can do whatever you want.

ALINA: What?

BACCHAE 1: You can do whatever you want.

Pause.

ALINA: Oh. That's. Wow.

BACCHAE 1: Yeah.

EIGHT: EPISODE 4

The GIRLS *are wearing ankle-tracking devices.* LUCKY *is looking at their computer.*

LUCKY: *Oh my god!*

LUCKY *is staring at their computer in disbelief.*

ELLE: What?! What happened? Is it Alina?

LUCKY: *Oh my god!*

CLEO: What?!

LUCKY: [*scrolling, reading*] Oh my god, oh my god, oh my god, oh my god … It can't … It can't be true …

ELLE: What is it? What's going on?

LUCKY: It's true. It's really true …

ELLE: Tell us! You have to tell us! *Tell us!*

Pause.

LUCKY: [*looking up*] I passed.

Silence.

I passed my Maths test. I passed. I'm not going to fail.

Pause. Everyone is staring at LUCKY, *annoyed.*

Sorry. But I passed. I passed the test!

    Silence. LUCKY *looks around expectantly.*

It's a good thing.

DYLAN: That's great. We're all happy for you.

LUCKY: Thanks.

    Silence.

My mum's gonna be so happy.

    Silence.

I just really can't believe it.

ELLE: Can you please shut up?

LUCKY: Whoa. Somebody's cranky.

ELLE: Just, I don't really give a shit about how anyone did on a stupid test right now, okay. Like who cares about any of that?

LUCKY: Okay okay, sorry.

ROB: I feel like crap.

ELLE: Me too.

ROB: I feel so guilty.

ELLE: Me too.

REX: For what?

ELLE: For like. Being here, when Alina is … out there.

REX: Yeah well don't. She made her choice.

ROB: You don't get it.

REX: And *you* get it?

ROB: Yes. I get it.

REX: Whatever.

CLEO: This thing is itching my ankle. I can't handle it.

ELLE: Don't play with it, you'll set it off.

REX: If you damage it you have to pay a fine.

CLEO: I think I have a rash under it.

DYLAN: I know how to get it off.

ROB: What?

DYLAN: I can get it off—you just need a pencil.

CLEO: Really?

DYLAN: Yeah. I saw it on YouTube.

CLEO: Do it.

DYLAN: Okay, come here.

REX: Are you insane? What are you doing?

CLEO: Um. No. I'm not insane. I'm just not in to mandatory fashion accessories.

> DYLAN *pops off the bracelet.*

Oh my god, this is amazing.

REX: Oh god, oh god, oh god …

CLEO: My ankle feels so free.

DYLAN: What should I do with this?

CLEO: Smash it.

REX: Don't smash it! It will set it off and the police will be here within thirty seconds.

CLEO: Oh yeah?

REX: Yeah.

DYLAN: Within thirty seconds?

REX: Yeah.

DYLAN: Not possible.

REX: Yes, it is possible.

DYLAN: Not in thirty seconds.

CLEO: Yeah, what are they like just hiding in the toilet right now?

ELLE: I'm taking mine off too.

> *She does.*

REX: Look, I don't know how long it will take but they will come here and we will all get in trouble. So just don't smash it, okay. You're lucky I'm not reporting you.

ELLE: *What?!*

REX: Nothing.

CLEO: No. Wait. You're going to report us?

REX: You are doing this in my presence even though I'm clearly uncomfortable with it! Even though it implicates me! It's actually, yeah, it's actually really unfair!

ELLE: You know what's unfair? Someone monitoring my every move.

REX: It's for your own—

ELLE: And someone erecting a giant fence keeping my friend from ever coming home.

REX: I mean. It's to keep you in.

ELLE: Why do I need to be kept in?!

REX: It's just difficult to trust any young, you know, um, woman, when—

ELLE: I'm going to punch you in the face.

DYLAN *stops* ELLE.

DYLAN: Whoa. Whoa. I mean I get the impulse, but maybe don't.

Pause.

CLEO: I think …

ELLE: What?

CLEO: I think we need to do something.

DYLAN: What do you mean?

CLEO: Like. Do something. About this. Instead of just sitting around arguing about it.

ELLE: Like what?

CLEO: Go. Into the bush.

REX: Uh. No.

DYLAN: That's a terrible idea.

ROB: Besides. I can't. It's just for girls.

CLEO: Gender is a freaking construct, Rob. You can do whatever you want.

DYLAN: Preach.

CLEO: This whole thing is bullshit. Building a *fence* for our *safety*? We don't need a *fence*. We need people to actually just talk to us like *human beings*.

ROB: You're right. We need to go find Alina.

LUCKY: You just have a crush on her.

ROB: No I don't.

LUCKY: Yes you do. He does. He's always had a crush on her.

ROB: I don't have a crush on her.

LUCKY: Then why'd you get her a Christmas present?

ROB: Uh. 'Cause it was Christmas?

ELLE: You got her a Christmas present?

LUCKY: Oh, please. You didn't get anyone else here a Christmas present.

DYLAN: Yeah, I didn't get a Christmas present.

CLEO: What'd you get her?

LUCKY: He got her this like little necklace with a rabbit pendant.

ELLE: You got her jewellery?

ROB: She likes rabbits.

DYLAN: That's so like—romance territory. Oh my god.

ROB: Look. Shut up. Who cares? I'm just saying our friend, someone we know, *someone we know personally*, is on the other side of that fence. And maybe I'm totally in love with her, sure, maybe, whatever, but that has nothing to do with the fact that we should be helping her.

REX: No-one knows what's really going on out there.

CLEO: So what? That means we like just pretend it's not happening? Just stay safe in our warm little houses and like live our lives and eat our sushi and like play Pokemon Go?

DYLAN: No-one plays Pokemon Go.

LUCKY: I mean some people play it. A few people … I've seen them.

CLEO: We need to do something. We need to *do* something. *We need to do something!*

LUCKY: What? What are we supposed to do? We're sixteen.

ELLE: That didn't stop Joan of Arc.

REX: Joan of Arc was schizophrenic.

ELLE: *You don't know that!*

CLEO: We don't have to accept everything that is thrown at us. We don't have to accept this wall.

ELLE: Yes! I don't want to be the person who just watched history happen. I want to be in the thick of it. I want to be part of the cause.

REX: What cause? They haven't made any statement!

ELLE: They made a thousand statements that no-one listened to. And so they exited. And now people are listening.

REX: But why? I don't see any problem. We're fine.

ELLE: Maybe *you* are fine, Rex, but the whole world isn't fine.

LUCKY: But what are we supposed to do about it?

ELLE: I don't know. But the first step is getting people's attention.

DYLAN: I have a Maths test tomorrow.

CLEO: *Screw your Maths test!*

LUCKY: My mum is gonna be here in like—

CLEO: *Screw your mum!*

LUCKY: Don't say that about my mum! Only I can say things about my mum. You know—

CLEO: Okay okay okay, sorry. I'm just saying. We need to. Just. Take action.

LUCKY: It won't make a difference.

REX: It will make a difference. You'll be arrested.

ELLE: I'm going. You all can do whatever you want, but I'm going. I'm tired of just obeying rules that make no sense to me.

CLEO: It's just on the other side of the fence. Just right over there. We've been in that bush a hundred times before. What could be so scary about it?

ROB tosses the chair over.

LUCKY: Dude! What are you doing?

ROB: I'm sick of sitting in this stupid chair!

DYLAN: Awesome.

Pause.

LUCKY: Yeah!

LUCKY tosses their chair over too.

DYLAN: Do that again and I'll snapchat it.

LUCKY: I'm not doing it again.

ELLE: I'm sick of these stupid ankle bracelets.

ELLE stomps on the ankle bracelet.

REX: No, don't!

An alarm goes off.

VOICE: ERROR 560. Tracking device damaged. Do not relocate. Remain until authorities arrive. ERROR 560. Tracking device damaged. Do not relocate. Remain until authorities arrive. ERROR 560. Tracking device damaged. Do not relocate. Remain until authorities arrive …

They all look at each other.

They run.

NINE: ODE 4

The BACCHAE *in the bush. Someone is reading a magazine. Someone is giving someone else a tattoo. Someone is tending the fire. Someone is painting their nails. Someone is reading feminist literature. Someone is making sandwiches.*

ALINA *stands watching. Fidgeting. Discontent.*

BACCHAE 4: [*reading the magazine*] You're Sagittarius, right?

BACCHAE 3: Yeah.

BACCHAE 4: It says, 'Be wary of deception from others and of your own tendency to become an easy victim of this deception. Several short trips are necessary now, but this may involve a dispute. The experience may be not altogether pleasant. Revisiting the past or rummaging through old photographs could be exactly what you need to do right now.'

BACCHAE 3: What month is this from?

BACCHAE 4: August.

BACCHAE 3: That's already happened.

BACCHAE 2: Does anyone else want a sandwich?

BACCHAE 5: What kind?

BACCHAE 2: We only have tuna.

BACCHAE 5: Ugh. No.

>ALINA *is still fidgeting.*

ALINA: I'll have one.

BACCHAE 2: Here, take this one. I'll make a new one.

>ALINA *chews.*

ALINA: Thanks.

>*She chews more.*

So.

>*She chews.*

BACCHAE 3: What?

ALINA: So we're just hanging out?

BACCHAE 3: What?

ALINA: What are we doing?

BACCHAE 3: What do you mean?

ALINA: We're just sitting here doing nothing? That's what we're doing?

BACCHAE 5: We're not doing nothing. [*Name*] is making a fire, [*name*] is reading [*title of a magazine*], [*name*] is reading [*title of a book*], [*name*] just made you a sandwich, [*name*] is off swimming in the river, and I'm about to take a nap.

ALINA: Yeah, but …

BACCHAE 5: But what?

ALINA: Like. Where are the wild rituals? Where are the drugs and sex? Where is the *rage*?

BACCHAE 3: I mean. You can do those things if you want. No-one's stopping you.

ALINA: What even is Dionysus?

Pause.

BACCHAE 1: I think Dionysus is like. Freedom.

BACCHAE 4: Totally. Freedom from like.

BACCHAE 1: All of it.

BACCHAE 4: *Yes!*

BACCHAE 1: All of the stuff.

BACCHAE 4: Exactly.

ALINA: So you're here. Just. Like. Doing freedom?

BACCHAE 1: I guess so.

ALINA: Well, I don't see how that's going to work.

BACCHAE 5: I mean. It's sort of already working.

BACCHAE 4: Yeah. I feel better.

BACCHAE 3: It's really nice out here.

ALINA: I mean sure. But. Like. All of it. The stuff. It's still going on. Back there. Back home.

BACCHAE 1: Yeah. So?

ALINA: Don't you see? We could *change* things.

BACCHAE 1: I don't see how.

BACCHAE 2: No-one cares what we think.

BACCHAE 1: I even had a YouTube channel.

BACCHAE 2: We all had YouTube channels. No-one listened.

BACCHAE 4: Yes. We spoke. We said things. We wrote things. We sang things. No-one listened.

BACCHAE 1: People like the way it is.

BACCHAE 4: They like their daughters quiet. They like their secrets secret. They like their place at the table.

ALINA: Yes. I know. But now we are together. And now they are scared. They are on the edge of the seats with fear. Do you know what they're saying?

BACCHAE 4: No. What are they saying?

ALINA: They're saying we're possessed. We're sick. We're murderers. Thieves. Witches. They are saying we have gone wild. And they are terrified the infection will spread.

BACCHAE 3: But. We're just camping.

BACCHAE 1: I brought an air mattress and clay face masks.

ALINA: Listen: Right now, back there, the rules are the same. They are thinking the same thoughts they always have. Making the same laws they always have. But they are worried. They are worried now. Which means …

BACCHAE 4: What?

ALINA: Which means now is the time for change.

BACCHAE 4: But how?

ALINA: We go back and make them look at our dirty faces. We tell them the truth. We make them see us and hear us and rearrange the world.

Pause.

BACCHAE 3: Yes.

Pause.

We tell them in all their effort to keep us safe, they have actually hurt us.

BACCHAE 1: Yes. We aren't hurting ourselves. We know what we need. We know what we want.

BACCHAE 5: They just aren't listening.

BACCHAE 1: They think they know me better than I know myself.

BACCHAE 4: They think I am stupid and silly.

ALINA: *Yes!* But they are wrong.

Pause.

BACCHAE 3: Okay.

BACCHAE 5: Okay.

ALINA: Okay.

BACCHAE 4: So?

Pause.

BACCHAE 3: Let's go.

TEN: EPISODE 5

ELLE: We ran through the city. Along the smooth pavement, past Target and the Shell station.

BACCHAE: We got up off the ground and turned towards home. It felt strange and familiar at the same time.

ELLE: Past Cotton On and Nando's. We stopped for a second, hearts pounding, at the pedestrian crossing, and pressed the button and waited in silence for the little green person to flash and then we kept running.

BACCHAE: We climbed the hill and waded through the shallow part of the river. Our feet got muddy. We felt electric.

ELLE: Houses, trees, a big truck with Woolworth's written on the side of it, street lamps, billboards, an old man getting out of his car.

BACCHAE: Branches, rocks, something moving in the bushes, it's best to ignore those sounds and keep going.

ELLE: We whipped past the shopping centre and aimed ourselves towards the bush. We figured, we figured we'd save the world.

LUCKY: Our friend.

ROB: We figured we'd save our friend.

ELLE: And maybe, maybe also the world.

BACCHAE: We were deliberate in our steps, crunching leaves, fog in the distance, we headed towards the future. Towards our plan to save the world.

No, not the world.

Ourselves.

The world.

Ourselves and maybe also the world.

ROB: We arrive on the outskirts of town. The bush. But the bush is now surrounded by a tall foreboding fence. We stood still and stared up at it.

BACCHAE: It's big and grey and ugly and there's no way around it.

LUCKY: They finished it.

BACCHAE: We stare.

Someone says:

I don't think we can climb this.

ALINA: Maybe we're stuck.

ELLE: We're stuck here forever.

REX: Someone sat on the ground.

BACCHAE: And someone shouted:

This is bullshit!

ROB: Someone shouted:

ELLE: *Alina!*

ALINA: I heard my name. *What?! Hello?! Is someone there?! On the other side?!*

ROB: *Alina?!*

ALINA: *Yes! I'm here! Who is that?!*

ROB: *It's Rob. And Elle!*

LUCKY: *And Lucky and Rex and Dylan!*

CLEO: *And Cleo!*

ELLE: *All of us! We came to find you!*

ALINA: *Here I am!*

DYLAN: *What are you doing?!*

ALINA: *Nothing much!*

DYLAN: *That's cool, that's cool!*

ALINA: *How are you all?!*

LUCKY: *I passed Maths!*

ALINA: *Congrats!*

LUCKY: *My mum is gonna be so happy when—!*

CLEO: *Alina, are you okay?!*

ALINA: *Yes! We're all here though! We're trying to come back home!*

ELLE: *What?!*

ALINA: *We're coming back! All of us! We are bringing Dionysis home!*

CLEO: *What's Dionysis?!*

ALINA: *Dionysis is an idea!*

BACCHAE: *A revolt!*

   Against how it is!

   The stuff!

ALINA: *We are gonna change things! If we can get over this dumb wall!*

ELLE: *I hate this wall!*

ALINA: *Me too!*

ELLE: *If you get over it, I am gonna join you!*

ALINA: *What?!*

ELLE: *If you get over the wall I am going to join your Dionysus thing!*

CLEO: *Me too! I'm going to join too!*

REX: I'm really uncomfortable with all of this.

CLEO: *Rex is not going to join you but that's okay, we don't need him!*

ELLE: *We miss you!*

ALINA: I'm gonna climb it.

BACCHAE: It's not possible.

ALINA: *Wait there! I'm climbing over!*

> ALINA *tries to climb the fence. When she touches it, she is electrocuted. Sparks fly. She falls to the ground. She is dead. An alarm sounds.*

VOICE: Perimeter has been breached. Please remain a safe distance from barrier. A safe distance is a distance of at least two meters. Thank you.

> *Blackout.*

ELEVEN: ODE 5

MESSENGER 3: We are watching from our window.

MESSENGER 2: We live across the street from Coles.

MESSENGER 3: Yeah.

MESSENGER 2: We are watching from our window as a group of girls and a group of kids I only sort of know meet at the fence.

MESSENGER 3: They are shouting at each other. I can't hear what they are saying.

MESSENGER 2: They are shouting and then it happens.

MESSENGER 3: She tries to climb the fence.

MESSENGER 2: She tries to climb the fence. And when she touches it her arms and legs flail out like she's falling. Like she's falling from the sky and reaching, reaching out for something to hold on to. And then she falls to the ground and is still.

MESSENGER 3: I hold my breath.

MESSENGER 2: It's an electric fence.

MESSENGER 3: I open the window and lean out.

MESSENGER 2: They are all staring at her body. Just laying in the dirt and grass and leaves.

MESSENGER 3: People are very, very still. And everyone gathers around her for a moment. Staring. On the other side of the fence people are confused. Someone is shouting questions. They can't see. They don't know she's dead.

MESSENGER 2: And I am calling for our mother.

MESSENGER 3: And I am telling you to shut up and keep watching.

MESSENGER 2: And then.

MESSENGER 3: Then.

MESSENGER 2: Well. The moment explodes.

MESSENGER 3: Everyone realises the fence is electric, and the electric fence is separating them. That they have no way of getting to each other. We are all stuck on our respective sides.

MESSENGER 2: Some of them start yelling. And people are coming out of their houses to see what's happening. Everyone starts throwing things at the fence. Sticks and rocks and furniture and whatever they can find.

MESSENGER 3: The girls in the bush are building a bonfire, the biggest one I've ever seen, the smoke is like a giant black snake slithering into the sky. They are lighting sticks on fire and throwing them at the fence.

MESSENGER 2: And everything is suddenly different. The air is different.

MESSENGER 3: I feel like this is the truest moment I've ever lived. I want to run outside and throw things. I want to smash the world into a thousand pieces.

MESSENGER 2: But you don't.

MESSENGER 3: I don't because you stop me.

MESSENGER 2: You weren't thinking.

MESSENGER 3: I look at you and you are filming it all on your phone. You're filming it all on your phone and I—

MESSENGER 2: You grab the phone out of my hands.

MESSENGER 3: I grab the phone out of your hands and I throw it—

MESSENGER 2: You throw it out the window.

MESSENGER 3: And you swear at me. You call me—

MESSENGER 2: I know. I'm sorry.

MESSENGER 3: I know.

MESSENGER 2: And the kids in town are running through the streets smashing windows and screaming at the top of their lungs.

MESSENGER 3: I want to join them.

MESSENGER 2: But we don't.

MESSENGER 3: We just watch. We witness.

MESSENGER 2: And it's so terrible, what's happening, but I'm floating on the outside of it like a ghost. It's just a fact. Something that happened once. A story that makes you shake your head and say, 'That's awful, that's so cruel, that should never happen', but it's just a story, it's not real, it's just some piece of history that you aren't attached to at all. This is like that. Except we are there.

MESSENGER 3: And I can't tell if it's on purpose or an accident, but the bonfire is getting out of control. It's starting to spread out on either side. It's spreading into the bush and into the town. People are running from it, they are flinging themselves into water for protection.

MESSENGER 2: We run to the river. We stand in the river and watch the world turn to soot around us.

MESSENGER 3: The fire rages faster and faster and larger and larger across the land. It eats the fence. The fence is gone.

MESSENGER 2: It burns for seven days and seven nights—

MESSENGER 3: Which is a week.

MESSENGER 2: In that week the fire smashes everything it touches. Chain stores, the post office, petrol stations, cars, houses, everything. There's nothing left. It's terrible.

MESSENGER 3: We watch while we sit with our feet in the water, waiting, waiting—

MESSENGER 2: And then.

MESSENGER 3: And then on the seventh night.

MESSENGER 2: On the seventh night—

MESSENGER 3: On the seventh night it begins to rain, and finally the fire sizzles and dies.

MESSENGER 2: Tired steam is rolling over the ground as people come out of hiding. The kids in the town and the kids in the bush are stumbling out of rivers and basements, broken, sooty, bloody, tired, and they are making their way back to the fence.

MESSENGER 3: But the fence is gone. Burnt to nothing.

MESSENGER 2: A pile of ash.

MESSENGER 3: All that's left is them.

MESSENGER 2: A group of people.

MESSENGER 3: Two groups of people.

MESSENGER 2: On either side of a fence that no longer stands.

MESSENGER 3: Two groups of people with nothing left.

MESSENGER 2: And.

MESSENGER 3: And they step over the black and meet each other. They stand and look around. And they realise.

MESSENGER 2: They have to start over.

    And so they do.

MESSENGER 3: We all do.

The KIDS *and the* BACCHAE *are bloody and sooty and broken and tired. They stand staring out at the audience. The* MESSENGERS *join them. They are united.*

TWELVE: EPISODE 6

There is no blackout between scenes Eleven and Twelve. The FULL CAST *stand facing the audience.*

ALL: And so
    it's dawn now,
    the horizon is soft and pink.
    It's cold and wet.
    A blue vault forms above us.
    I'm barely awake.
    I've hardly made a dent.
    I'm still in bed.
    There are eternities ahead
    of me.
    Me resting.
    Me waiting.
    Me gathering myself.

    We have only possibility in our pockets.

    We can expand or tax the sky
    we can save or scorch the earth
    we can learn to fly or we can drown
    but we will birth
    a new world.
    Filled with objects you can't fathom.
    Ideas you can't imagine.
    We make no promises
    because we know
    promises are fragile.
    They break.
    But we will charge forward
    with hope
    swirling beneath our skin.

THIRTEEN: EXODOS

Again, no blackout. Thirteen is a continuation of Twelve which is a continuation of Eleven.

VIOLET *begins to perform the same song from the first scene. The sun rises.* VIOLET *performs the song through to the end.*

THE END

www.currency.com.au

Visit Currency Press' website now to:

- Buy your books online
- Browse through our full list of titles, from plays to screenplays, books on theatre, film and music, and more
- Choose a play for your school or amateur performance group by cast size and gender
- Obtain information about performance rights
- Find out about theatre productions and other performing arts news across Australia
- For students, read our study guides
- For teachers, access syllabus and other relevant information
- Sign up for our email newsletter

The performing arts publisher